T 403974

Louisiana

by Jason Glaser

Consultant:
Robert Rome
Louisiana Council
for Social Studies

Mankato, Minnesota

Capstone Press
151 Good Counsel Drive • P.O. Box 669 • Mankato, Minnesota 56002
http://www.capstone-press.com

Copyright © 2003 by Capstone Press. All rights reserved.
No part of this publication may be reproduced in whole or in part, or stored in a retrieval system, or transmitted in any form or by any means, electronic, mechanical, photocopying, recording, or otherwise, without written permission of the publisher.
For information regarding permission, write to Capstone Press,
151 Good Counsel Drive, P.O. Box 669, Dept. R, Mankato, Minnesota 56002.
Printed in the United States of America

Library of Congress Cataloging-in-Publication Data
Glaser, Jason.
    Louisiana / by Jason Glaser.
    p. cm.—(Land of liberty)
    Summary: Provides an overview of the state of Louisiana, covering its history, geography, government, economy, people, and culture. Includes a recipe for pecan pralines.
    Includes bibliographical references and index.
    ISBN 0-7368-1586-4 (hardcover)
    1. Louisiana—Juvenile literature. [1. Louisiana.] I. Title. II. Series.
F369.3.G56 2003
976.3—dc21   2002010321

Editorial Credits
Brad Hoehn, editor; Christopher Harbo, editor; Eric Kudalis, product planning editor; Jennifer Schonborn, series and book designer; Angi Gahler, illustrator; Kelly Garvin, photo researcher

Photo Credits
Cover images: Jungle Gardens at Avery Island, Houserstock/Jan Butchofsky; City of New Orleans, PhotoDisc
Bart Kemper, 38, 40–41
Capstone Press/Gary Sundermeyer, 54
Corbis/Buddy Mays, 32; Philip Gould, 36; Robert Holmes, 30–31
Doug Perrine/Seapics.com, 14
Houserstock/Dave G. Houser, 4, 16–17, 42, 45, 49, 56, 63; Jan Butchofsky, 46
Hulton Archive by Getty Images, 28
Index Stock Imagery/Frank Staub, 8
Louisiana Office of Tourism, 6, 12, 43, 52, 53, 57
Huey Long Photo Album, Louisiana Division, New Orleans Public Library, 37
North Wind Picture Archives, 18, 20–21
One Mile Up, Inc, 55 (both)
PhotoDisc, 1
Stock Montage, Inc, 22, 25, 26, 58
U.S. Postal Service, 59

Artistic Effects
Louisiana Office of Tourism

1 2 3 4 5 6   08 07 06 05 04 03

Table of Contents

Chapter 1	About Louisiana	5
Chapter 2	Land, Climate, and Wildlife	9
Chapter 3	History of Louisiana	19
Chapter 4	Government and Politics	33
Chapter 5	Economy and Resources	39
Chapter 6	People and Culture	47
Maps	Louisiana Cities	7
	Louisiana's Land Features	11
Features	Recipe: Praline Pecans	54
	Louisiana's Flag and Seal	55
	Almanac	56
	Timeline	58
	Words to Know	60
	To Learn More	61
	Internet Sites	61
	Places to Write and Visit	62
	Index	64

People ride floats through the streets of New Orleans during Mardi Gras parades. They throw cups, beads, and candy to the crowds.

Chapter 1

About Louisiana

More than one million people come to New Orleans, Louisiana, each year to take part in the "Greatest Free Show on Earth." People have celebrated Mardi Gras in Louisiana for more than 300 years.

Mardi Gras is French for "Fat Tuesday." The celebration is held 47 days before Easter Sunday. The Monday before Mardi Gras is called Lundi Gras. Both are Louisiana holidays.

During the two weeks before Mardi Gras, carnival groups called "krewes" hold parades, carnival balls, and parties in New Orleans. Krewe members wear costumes and ride through the streets on floats. Krewes hand out toys, beads, fake coins, and candy.

Bead colors are an important part of Mardi Gras costumes. In 1782, the king of the Mardi Gras chose the official bead colors of purple, green, and gold. Purple stands for justice, green stands for faith, and gold stands for power.

Pelican State

Louisiana is a southern state. Texas borders it on the west. Arkansas lies to the north. The Mississippi River forms the border between Louisiana and the state of Mississippi on the east. The Gulf of Mexico lies to the south.

One of Louisiana's nicknames is the "Pelican State." A pelican and its chicks appear on Louisiana's state seal. William Charles Cole Claiborne was the first governor of Louisiana. He thought the pelican showed how well the state took care of its people.

The eastern brown pelican is Louisiana's state bird.

Spanish moss grows on the trees in Louisiana's bayous.

Chapter 2

Land, Climate, and Wildlife

Two of Louisiana's bordering waters affect the climate and soil of the state. The Gulf of Mexico brings in warm air and moisture. This air keeps Louisiana hot in the summer and warm the rest of the year. The Mississippi River brings in silt, a rich soil that helps plants grow. Both bordering waters are important to Louisiana's Gulf Coastal Region, Mississippi River Alluvial Plain, and the West Gulf Coastal Plain.

The Gulf Coastal Region

The Gulf Coastal Region includes the southeastern states from Florida to Texas. The Gulf of Mexico keeps these areas warm.

> *"It's home. You just get that feeling when you're there, just a warm feeling inside. That's all that matters."*
> —Britney Spears, singer, about Kentwood, Louisiana

The Gulf Coastal Region is made of several smaller regions. Three of those regions lie partly within Louisiana. The small area of Louisiana east of the Mississippi River and north of Lake Pontchartrain is part of the East Gulf Coastal Plain. The size of this area is 3,500 square miles (9,065 square kilometers). It is filled with marshes that lie barely above sea level.

The Mississippi River Alluvial Plain

The area around the Mississippi River, from the top of the state to the Gulf of Mexico, is the Mississippi River Alluvial Plain. Sand, dirt, and other materials rivers carry from upstream are called alluvial deposits. These deposits increase the land size. Most of Louisiana was created thousands of years ago by the Mississippi River deposits.

The river's path changes over time. Each time the river changes, it leaves behind a slow moving body of water called a delta or bayou. The bayous are filled with cypress trees covered with a thick growth called Spanish moss.

Sometimes the Mississippi River bends and reconnects with itself. When the water flows back through the connection, it leaves behind bodies of water called oxbow lakes.

The water flowing through the Mississippi River Alluvial Plain has carved much of the land. Many areas are now below sea level. New Orleans is one of the few U.S. cities located below sea level. People in the city build walls called levees to prevent flooding.

Visitors to Kisatchie National Forest can explore rivers and bayous along 100 miles (161 kilometers) of hiking trails. Kisatchie National Forest is in Louisiana's West Gulf Coastal Plain.

The West Gulf Coastal Plain

The far west and northwestern areas of Louisiana are called the West Gulf Coastal Plain. This region has the highest elevation in Louisiana. Louisiana's only mountain, Driskill Mountain, is 535 feet (163 meters) above sea level.

This area has several forests and state parks. The Kisatchie National Forest covers about 600,000 acres (243,000 hectares). The forest is split among six areas in the northern and central parts of the state. About 90 percent of the remaining forests are privately owned. In the early 1900s, many Louisiana forests were cut down. People bought land in forest areas to keep the pine and oak trees from disappearing.

Marshlands cover the coastal section of the West Gulf Coastal Plain. These marshlands mix freshwater river runoff with saltwater from the Gulf of Mexico. Salt marshes are home to fish, shellfish, and plants important to the Louisiana economy.

Did you know...?
Louisiana has 3 million acres (1,200,000 hectares) of wetlands. About 40 percent of all of the salt marshes in the United States are found in Louisiana.

Kemp's Ridley Sea Turtle

The Kemp's Ridley Sea Turtle is one of the smallest sea turtles. They often live for more than 30 years and weigh less than 100 pounds (45 kilograms). Their shells are about 25 inches (65 centimeters) long. These turtles eat fish, shellfish, and crabs.

In Louisiana, many Kemp's Ridley Sea Turtles drown when they are caught in shrimp nets. Pollution also harms the turtles' habitat.

In 1947, more than 40,000 female Kemp's Ridley Sea Turtles nested. By the end of 2000, less than 200 remained. In recent years, scientists in Louisiana have worked hard to protect the turtles. They believe only about 900 female turtles are alive today.

Salt Domes and Barrier Islands

Louisiana's Gulf Coast Region has rich salt and petroleum deposits. When the land formed, large salt deposits were trapped under the soil. Over time, petroleum and other natural gasses developed and pushed up on the salt deposits.

"It has wildlife from egrets to alligators and other swamp life. And the Tabasco plant is there. I always ask for Tabasco everywhere I go, whether I use it or not. It makes me feel comfortable."
—Faith Ford, actress, born in Louisiana

These salt dome areas are heavily mined for salt. Petroleum is mined for fuel.

Louisiana's barrier islands protect the state's southern coastline from strong weather. Strong winds and rainstorms travel up the Gulf of Mexico. These storms damage the southern area of Louisiana. The barrier islands act as a shield against large storms and hurricanes.

Water Life and Wetlands

Various forms of water life make their homes in Louisiana's wetlands. Louisiana is famous for the shrimp, crawfish, oysters, and catfish that are raised and harvested each year.

More than 400 bird species live in Louisiana's wetlands. Many birds feed off large supplies of wetland shrimp and fish. Pelicans, gulls, and sandpipers are among the birds that live along Louisiana's coast.

Alligators and snapping turtles live on the swampy bayous and freshwater wetlands. People hunt alligators for their skins. The skins are used to make products similar to leather.

Louisiana has many kinds of snakes, including the diamondback, speckled king snake, and western cottonmouth.

Many mammals make their homes in Louisiana's forests. Squirrels, foxes, opossums, skunks, otters, and raccoons are common in the western and northern forests. Deer, bobcats, and coyotes also live in the northern parts of the state

Environmental Problems

Louisiana's wetlands face many dangers. Hurricanes tear away soil and fish beds. Storms pollute freshwater areas with ocean

salt water, creating brackish water. Too much salt water can kill some fish and plants. People in Louisiana work year round to keep salt levels balanced by building protective areas.

About 25 to 35 square miles (65 to 91 square kilometers) of marshland disappear each year. Rivers are partly responsible for eating away the land areas. Channels dug for the oil and gas pipelines also cut into the wetlands.

The wetlands are home to several endangered species, including the loggerhead sea turtle and the glossy ibis. These animals may be saved if people can protect the wetlands.

Louisiana's swamps and bayous are home to many alligators. This alligator lives in Atchafalaya, North America's largest river swamp.

In 1682, French fur trader René-Robert Cavelier, known as Sieur de La Salle, claimed the Louisiana area for France.

Chapter 3

History of Louisiana

Spain was the first country to claim the land that today is Louisiana. In 1519, Alonso Alvarez de Pineda explored the Gulf Coast from Florida to Texas. Pineda was a mapmaker who claimed this entire area for Spain.

French Explorers

René-Robert Cavalier, known as Sieur de La Salle, was a French fur trader from Canada. In the late 1600s, he was looking for river routes for trade. He traveled along the Detroit River before taking the Mississippi River into the Louisiana area. In 1682, he claimed the area for France. He called it Louisiana in honor of King Louis XIV of France.

La Salle founded areas that later became Louisiana cities. In one location, he saw a red stick poking out of a hillside. This stick marked Indian hunting grounds. His fellow explorers called the area Baton Rouge, which means "red stick" in French.

In the early 1700s, French Canadian Louis Juchereau de Saint-Denis traveled from Canada to Louisiana. The French governor, Father Francisco Hidalgo, worried about a Spanish attack. Saint-Denis helped build Fort Saint Jean Baptiste. Later named Natchitoches, this fort was the first permanent settlement in the Louisiana area.

The French knew the Mississippi River would be helpful for travel and trade. They wanted to build a city near the mouth of the Mississippi. In 1718, the French formed New Orleans. The city was declared the capital in 1723. Citizens voted to move the capital to Baton Rouge in 1849.

Louisiana Changes Hands

In 1762, King Louis XV of France gave New Orleans and the land west of it to his cousin, King Charles III of Spain. In 1763, France turned over the area east of New Orleans to

In 1764, many French Canadians were forced out of Canada by the war between England and France. Today, descendants of these people are called Cajuns.

England through the Treaty of Paris. This treaty helped bring an end to the Seven Years War (1756–1763) between England and France.

In 1764, French Canadians known as Acadians arrived in Louisiana. During England's fight against France, the British had forced Acadians out of their Canadian lands. Mainly fishermen and farmers, Acadians did not trade with British or French traders. The Acadians had their own culture and form of the French language. Today, these people are called Cajuns.

Many settlers in Louisiana did not like either Spanish or British rule. The American settlers fought for their

French Emperor Napoleon I sold the Louisiana Territory to the United States for $15 million.

Free People of Color

In the early 1700s, slavery began in Louisiana. But not all African American people living in Louisiana were slaves. Many arrived in Louisiana following revolts in Haiti. Others bought their freedom while working in America. These people were called "Les Gens de Couleur Libres," or "Free People of Color." Many Free People owned property and were merchants. Others were doctors, teachers, or writers.

independence in the Revolutionary War (1775-1783). Louisiana soldiers helped keep Baton Rouge and other cities from being captured. After winning the war with England, Americans began to travel into Louisiana.

Spain and England believed they could no longer control the area. Control was returned to Emperor Napoleon I of France. In 1803, Napoleon sold the entire Louisiana Territory for $15 million to U.S. President Thomas Jefferson.

The State of Louisiana in Wartime

The Louisiana Purchase was divided into the District of Louisiana in the North and the Territory of Orleans in the South. In 1812, Louisiana, which had been the Territory of

Orleans, became the 18th state of the Union. Citizens chose William Charles Cole Claiborne as governor. Louisiana now also included the Baton Rouge area. This area had been part of Spanish Florida.

After selling Louisiana to the United States, France again went to war with Great Britain. Britain did not want the United States to do business with France. Britain blocked U.S. ships from meeting with French traders. The British sometimes took Americans from ships to fight for the British. In 1812, the United States declared war on Great Britain. This conflict is known as the War of 1812 (1812–1814).

British and U.S. soldiers fought this war in the northern U.S. states and in Canada. On December 24, 1814, the two countries declared peace. But news of the treaty did not reach all the soldiers right away. British soldiers attacked New Orleans in January 1815. U.S. troops led by General Andrew Jackson and the French pirate Jean LaFitte defeated them. The Battle of New Orleans was the Americans' greatest defeat of the British.

Civil War

When the U.S. Civil War (1861–1865) began, the people of Louisiana were not sure what side to take. Louisiana traded

On April 24, 1862, the Union ships captured New Orleans from the Confederate Army.

with the North, but also had ties with the South. In 1861, Louisiana declared itself an independent nation and seceded from the Union.

Two months later, Louisiana joined other southern states in the Confederacy. In 1862, Union forces captured New Orleans and much of Louisiana, which they controlled during the war. After the war ended, many former slaves moved to Louisiana. They took some of the jobs that had been held by Free People of Color.

Reconstruction

Following the Civil War, some people wanted to work with the Union and northern states to rebuild Louisiana. This was called Reconstruction. Other people wanted to stop northern control of Louisiana. Louisiana agreed to give up slavery, but did not allow African Americans to vote right away.

Louisiana's constitution of 1868 gave African American men in the state the right to vote.

Creole

Some people in Louisiana are called Creole. Creole was once used to describe the Free People of Color living in Louisiana. These free African Americans and former slaves spoke French and were descendants of the French.

Today, Creole usually refers to anyone in Louisiana with French or Spanish ancestors. Some people only use the term to refer to those whose ancestors came to Louisiana directly from France.

The word "Creole" sometimes is confused with "Cajun." Cajuns are the descendants of the French people who moved to Louisiana from Canada or the northern states.

During Reconstruction, projects to improve schools, housing, and sanitation began. These projects were not always handled equally for whites and African Americans.

In 1865, African Americans in Louisiana created the Convention of Colored Men. This group encouraged Louisiana to adopt a Black Code that gave African American men rights such as owning property. Northern states did not believe these codes were enough. The 1866 Civil Rights Act gave African Americans more rights. Many people in Louisiana fought these changes by rioting and damaging property. Whites formed groups like the Ku Klux Klan to frighten African Americans and keep them from exercising what rights they had.

Louisiana Industries

Reconstruction efforts hurt Louisiana's economy. Sugarcane plantations no longer had slave labor. Plantation owners had to pay living wages to free workers. Landowners began to use sharecroppers to tend and harvest their crops. Sharecroppers

In the early 1900s, children and adults harvested sugarcane on Louisiana's plantations.

gave half the crops to the landowner at harvest time. They then paid for the use of the land from the remaining half. Sharecroppers earned little profit from their hard work.

> **Did you know...?**
> During World War II, Higgins Industries made more than 20,000 Higgins Boats for Allied troops. Each boat could carry 36 soldiers and their equipment on each trip it made to shore.

Between 1880 and 1910, railroads were built. The railroads allowed Louisiana to sell more sugar to the north. The railroads also brought more travelers. People built restaurants and hotels. The forestry industry also began during this time.

After the discovery of oil in the early 1900s, workers sold oil to northern cities for car fuel. Oil money allowed Louisiana to build roads and highways. It also helped build and support manufacturing plants.

Louisiana's growing economy allowed the state to give money to World War I (1914–1918) and World War II (1939–1945) efforts. In World War II, a man named Andrew Higgins created a boat called the Landing Craft Vehicle Personnel (LCVP), also known as the Higgins Boat.

Higgins Boats carried and protected army forces. In order to make enough boats, Higgins employed women and African Americans of all ages at his New Orleans plant. The boats were used for the D-Day invasion of Europe during World War II.

New Beginnings

In the 1900s, equality between African Americans and whites improved in Louisiana. Louisiana began desegragating its schools in the 1950s and 1960s. Desegregation brought whites and African Americans together in schools and colleges. In 1977, New Orleans elected an African American mayor, Ernest "Dutch" Morial.

In the second half of the 20th century, Louisiana became a popular tourist spot. Millions of people visited New Orleans

for Mardi Gras, jazz festivals, and other attractions. New Orleans served as the site for the 1984 World's Fair.

Sporting events draw many tourists to Louisiana. In 1975, a football arena called the Superdome opened in New Orleans. Each year two college football teams play a game called the Sugar Bowl there. The New Orleans Saints NFL football team also plays in the dome. In 2002, the Super Bowl was held at the Superdome.

The New Orleans Saints started playing at the Superdome in 1975. Today, the Saints play eight regular season games in the dome each year.

The Louisiana State Capitol is the tallest state capitol in the United States. The building stands 450 feet (137 meters) tall.

Chapter 4

Government and Politics

Louisiana is divided into 64 parishes while other states have counties. When Louisiana was first settled, most of its people were Roman Catholic. The citizens of each town had a church. The area surrounding the church was called a parish. When Louisiana's government formed, it kept the parish divisions instead of making counties.

Each parish keeps legal records of its citizens, the land boundaries, and court documents. The parish form of government is called a "policy jury."

Since 1812, Louisiana has adopted 11 constitutions. Lawmakers call for a new constitution when they believe too

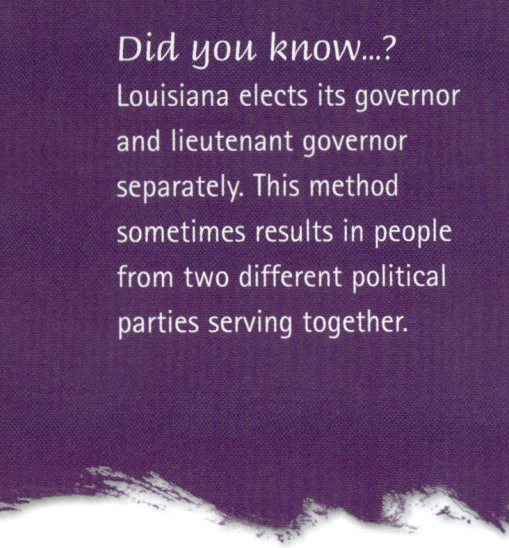

Did you know…?
Louisiana elects its governor and lieutenant governor separately. This method sometimes results in people from two different political parties serving together.

many changes to the old constitution are being suggested. The most recent constitution was adopted in 1974. It gives parishes power to make legal decisions that before only the state government could make.

Louisiana's Branches of Government

A governor heads Louisiana's executive branch. The governor is elected once every four years. Each governor can serve only two terms in a row. A person can be elected to the seat again after another governor's term has passed.

The legislative branch in Louisiana is shared by the state senate and state house of representatives. State senators and representatives are elected to four-year terms. The legislature creates and passes the laws that govern the state of Louisiana.

Louisiana courts make up the judicial branch of government. Judges are elected by the people. The courts use a system based on the Napoleonic Code. These laws existed in France when Napoleon was emperor. In other U.S. states, courts use a practice called "common law." Common law is guided by rulings from earlier court cases. In Louisiana, decisions are

Louisiana's State Government

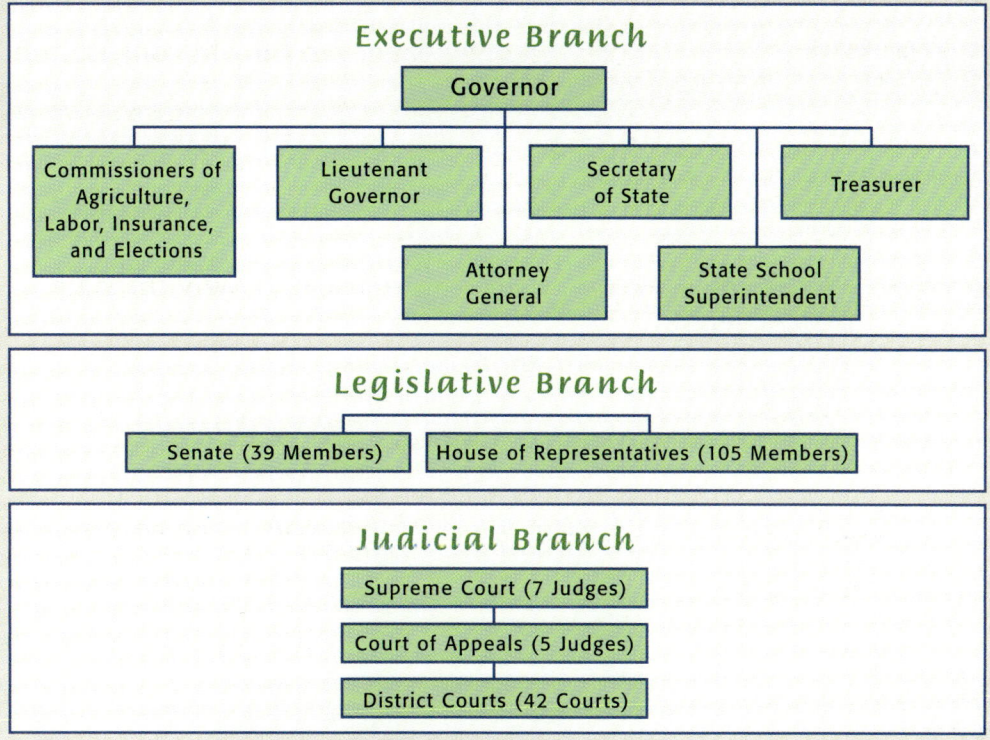

based on the current case. The outcome of a new case may not be the same as earlier rulings.

Louisiana's Political Position

Since the late 1800s, Democrats have controlled Louisiana politics. Louisiana politicians were called "Southern Democrats." Louisiana's members of the Democratic Party were usually more conservative than Democrats from other parts of the country.

Louisiana uses the open primary system for voting. In an open primary, all of the candidates from each political party run against each other. The top two candidates meet each other in a runoff.

Women are beginning to win elections in Louisiana. In 1991, Melinda Schwegmann was the first woman elected as lieutenant governor. In 1997, Mary Landrieu was the first woman elected for a full term as senator.

Melinda Schwegmann shakes hands with U.S. Representative William Jefferson. Melinda served as Louisiana's lieutenant governor from 1992 to 1995.

The Kingfish

Huey P. Long was a famous Louisiana politician. Elected governor in 1928, he promised to build better roads, hospitals, and schools. Long was popular among the people of Louisiana. People called him "the Kingfish," a character from a popular radio program.

Long made promises at the expense of Louisiana's rich. They tried to get him out of office by charging him with misuse of state funds. Long was smart and had many friends. He built a strong group of political partners who helped him stay in office.

Long's power allowed him to control most of Louisiana's government. He placed friends in certain positions because he knew they would follow his orders. In 1930, Long was elected to the U.S. Senate while he was still Louisiana's governor. From 1930 and 1932, he served as both senator and governor. In 1932, Long resigned as governor.

On September 8, 1935, Long met with state politicians in Baton Rouge. While there, a family member of one of his political enemies shot him. Long later died at the hospital. After his death, Long's wife and many of his relatives served in politics.

River barges carry grain, steel, and other products up and down the Mississippi River.

Chapter 5

Economy and Resources

Waterways affect Louisiana's economy. Six major railroads connect to the shipping port of New Orleans. It is one of the busiest ports in the United States.

Louisiana companies build many ships. Shipyard workers build oil tankers, cold storage ships, coast guard patrol boats, fishing ships, river barges, and tugboats. During wartime, Louisiana ship builders made warships for the Navy.

Oil and Gas

Louisiana is one of the largest oil producing states. In the early 1900s, oil was found under salt domes and under land covered by coastal water. Louisiana was the first state to build oil wells so far off shore they could not be seen from land.

Louisiana also produces other types of fuel. Natural gas is often found in the same underground deposits as oil. Some parts of Louisiana make and use a special kind of gasoline. This "gasohol fuel" is safer for the environment than gasoline.

Oil and natural gas are transported to the rest of the United States by oil tankers or pipelines. Oil tankers travel up the Mississippi River and dock at ports. The tankers then pump the fuel to tanker trucks for transport. Pipelines carry oil for refining to other areas of the United States. Louisiana

produces a large number of petrochemical products. Of these, rubber is the most common. Plastic, latex, fertilizer, and printing inks are other petrochemicals.

Agriculture and Forestry

Sugarcane is Louisiana's largest agricultural product. One of Louisiana's nicknames is "Sugar State." In the 1750s, pioneers began growing sugarcane. They cut and sold sugar stalks as snacks. By the 1800s, mill workers refined the sugarcane into sugar crystals much like the sugar sold today.

Many oil refineries are near the Mississippi River in Louisiana. Oil tankers from these refineries carry fuel up river to other ports.

Tourists visit the McIlhenny Company in Avery Island, Louisiana. This company makes Tabasco sauce.

Louisiana's hot weather is good for growing sweet potatoes. These yellow-orange, sweet-tasting potatoes grow best in near-tropical conditions. Louisiana's hot, wet weather is also good for growing rice, cotton, and pecans. Louisiana is the home of Tabasco, a seasoning, which comes from a hot pepper.

Louisiana has many oak, pine, and cypress forests. The Louisiana forest industry uses trees to make many products. Lumber is used for building materials. Lumber workers press sawdust together to make a building material called particleboard. Wood pulp is used to make paper, cellophane, and other products. Factories turn tree bark into glue and fertilizer. The Louisiana Forestry Association works with forest industries to replace trees cut down for lumber.

Fishing and Seafood

Shrimp is Louisiana's most profitable seafood industry. Shrimp makes up 85 percent of the seafood harvested in the state.

Fishermen use large nets to catch shrimp in Louisiana waters. More shrimp are caught in Louisiana than anywhere else in the United States.

"I see things like Cirque du Soleil and Riverdance and all the other first-class productions that go to Mississippi and we have the same kind of talent on the street corners of New Orleans."
—Melva Vallery, politician, Louisiana's 91st District

Louisiana's waters provide more than 7 million pounds of brown shrimp and white shrimp each year.

Crab fishing is a growing industry in Louisiana. Crab harvests sometimes are larger than harvests in the New England crab states. Louisiana fishers catch over 50 million pounds of crab each year.

Crawfish farming and oyster harvesting are also growing businesses in Louisiana. Fishers trap crawfish in rivers, swamps, and bayous. Farmers also raise crawfish in ponds. Most oysters in Louisiana are grown in a controlled mixture of saltwater and freshwater.

In freshwater areas, fishers catch and sell large amounts of catfish, a popular food in Louisiana. In saltwater areas, fishers catch flounder, mackerel, trout, groupers, and even sharks.

Tourism

Louisiana's culture attracts many people to the state each year. Tourists enjoy the warm weather and the hot, spicy Cajun and

Tourists enjoy visiting the French Quarter in New Orleans.

Creole cooking. Fishing is also a popular pastime. Each year, tourists spend more than $5 billion in Louisiana.

While Mardi Gras brings in the most tourists, Louisiana also offers other attractions. Travelers enjoy seeing the French Quarter in New Orleans. Performers juggle, dance, and play music for visitors walking along streets. Boats sail around New Orleans for passengers to view the city's sights from the river.

Musicians and street performers entertain people in New Orleans.

Chapter 6

People and Culture

Many groups of people have influenced Louisiana's population. French, British, Spanish, Haitian, and African ancestors created a special culture in Louisiana. Many Louisianans call themselves Creole or Cajun.

Louisiana's culture includes its food, music, schools, and language. French, English, and a mix of both languages can be heard in the streets and in people's homes.

Food

Louisiana is famous for spicy food. Tabasco sauce, made from locally grown peppers, is used on meat, vegetables, and even

Voodoo

Haitians brought traditions of voodoo with them to Louisiana. Voodoo is the name for a mystical faith and practice that developed in Haiti during the 1700s. Voodoo is a belief in nature spirits called the Loa. Practicing voodoo is meant to increase the energy in one's own spirit, called Kundalini.

The most famous Louisiana voodoo leader was Marie Laveau, a Free Person of Color born near the end of the 1700s. After she and her followers attended mass, she held religious ceremonies behind the local Catholic church. She called herself the Voodoo Queen and the Voodoo Pope. She had 15 children, some of whom also practiced voodoo.

in drinks. Many Louisiana-style recipes call for food to be "blackened." Cooks often rub these foods with spices and then char, or burn, them until the outside turns black.

Louisiana residents eat large amounts of local seafood. Many Louisiana dishes are made of shrimp, catfish, crawfish, crab, and oysters. Recipes use shrimp in soups, salads, stews, barbecues, and appetizers.

Traditional New Orleans cooking styles are popular around the country. Famous New Orleans chef Emeril Legasse has created a cooking show. Several of his cookbooks feature southern-style recipes.

People enjoy eating crawfish in Louisiana. These freshwater crustaceans are boiled and served whole.

Music

In the early 1900s, New Orleans became a music center. Caribbean, ragtime, gospel, African drums, Spanish guitars, and many other types of music became popular in the city. New Orleans is the birthplace of jazz. Jazz musicians still play in concerts, shows, and festivals in Louisiana and around the United States.

In the 1920s, the blues became popular among African American musicians. Louis Armstrong, a pioneer blues musician, was born in Louisiana. The blues are slower than jazz and have a heavier style.

Cajuns living near Lafayette developed fast-paced music known as zydeco. In the late 1940s, musicians played this popular music on an accordion and a ripple board called a washboard. People once used washboards to clean laundry by rubbing clothes over the board's ridges. A variation of zydeco uses fiddles and steel guitars.

Schools

Louisiana teachers earn one of the lowest average salaries of teachers in the United States. These low wages make it hard to bring new teachers to Louisiana. As a result, many teachers

Louisiana's Ethnic Background

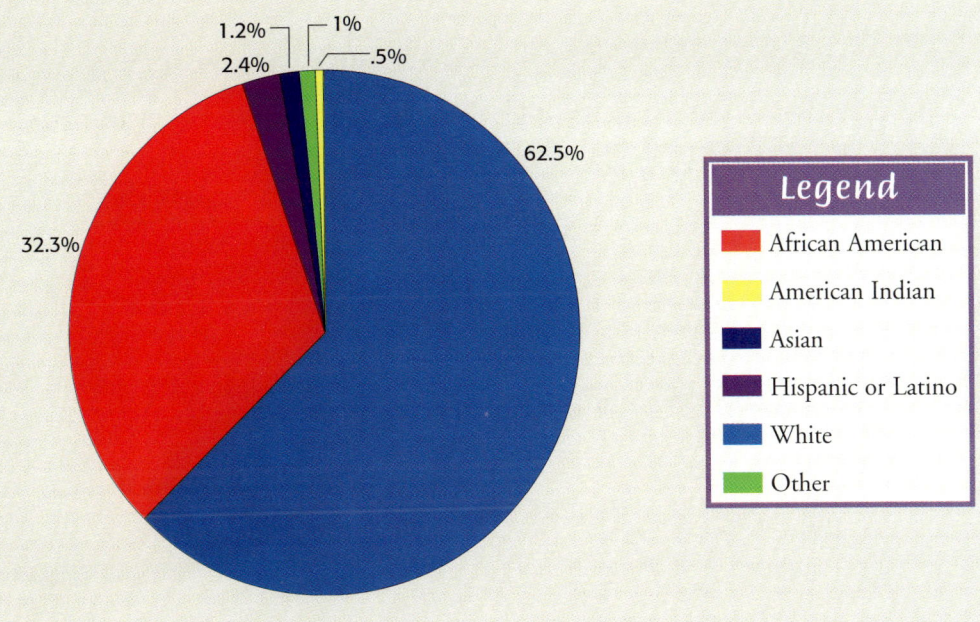

have had to teach large classes. Since the 1990s, the state has worked to correct this problem. Today, Louisiana limits elementary classes up to third grade to 18 students per teacher.

Louisiana educators are trying to improve education in the state. Schools have adopted higher graduation standards and focused on reading and math skills. Profits from the oil businesses are being invested in the school system.

Antebellum Mansions

Before the Civil War, large plantation farms in Louisiana were very profitable. Plantation owners built large mansions for their families. Smaller buildings for slaves surrounded the mansions. Other small buildings were used for cooking, blacksmithing, and other work. The plantation operated like a small village.

The mansions included large, round, or square columns of Greek design. Mansions often were painted white with green shutters or trim. Large windows held many panels of glass. Inside rooms usually featured bare walls, decorated ceilings, and only a few pieces of furniture. Most plantation owners kept a home in town, so the mansion on the plantation was often empty.

River Life

Steamboats have always been a popular way to travel in and around Louisiana. In the first part of the 1900s, they were used as a way to travel and transport cargo up and down the Mississippi River. Today, steamboats are used for sightseeing and tourism.

Steamboats are popular attractions in Louisiana. Gambling is legal on Louisiana's steamboats. The *Delta Queen* and other large steamboats are really traveling hotels. Guests have private rooms and can eat in onboard restaurants. The river features many places to see. Many of these places also offer guided fishing and sightseeing trips.

Louisiana's rivers and bayous are the backdrop for the state's rich history and culture. Beautiful wetlands, colorful Mardi Gras parades, and delicious Cajun cooking keep visitors coming back to the Pelican State each year.

The Delta Queen has traveled up and down the Mississippi River since 1947.

Recipe: Praline Pecans

Pecans became an important part of Louisiana's economy in the early 1800s. Today, praline pecans are a popular candy in Louisiana and other southern states.

Ingredients

1 egg white
1 teaspoon (5 mL) water
2 pounds (910 grams) pecan halves
1 cup (240 mL) sugar
1 teaspoon (5 mL) cinnamon
1 teaspoon (5 mL) salt
1 teaspoon (5 mL) cocoa

Equipment

nonstick cooking spray
9- by 13-inch (23- by 33-centimeter) baking pan
wire whisk
mixing bowls (2)
mixing spoons
measuring spoons
dry ingredient measuring cups
pot holders
spatula
waxed paper

What You Do

1. Preheat oven to 325°F (160°C).
2. Spray inside of baking pan with nonstick cooking spray. Set aside.
3. With wire whisk, beat egg white and water together in a bowl.
4. Quickly stir pecans into egg mixture with mixing spoon.
5. With clean mixing spoon, mix together sugar, cinnamon, salt, and cocoa in a second bowl.
6. Pour sugar mixture over pecans and stir quickly with mixing spoon.
7. Pour pecan mixture into prepared baking pan.
8. Bake 45 minutes. Stir every 10 minutes with mixing spoon. Clean mixing spoon between each stirring.
9. Carefully remove pan from oven using pot holders. Using spatula, loosen pecans immediately from the baking pan.
10. Let cool on waxed paper.

Makes 10–12 servings

Louisiana's Flag and Seal

Louisiana's Flag

Louisiana's state flag was adopted by the Louisiana Legislature in 1912. It is a blue flag with an eastern brown pelican tearing at its flesh to feed its young. The pelican represents the caring nature of Louisiana's government for its people. Louisiana's state motto, "Union, Justice and Confidence," is printed on a gold ribbon below the nest.

Louisiana's State Seal

Louisiana's state seal was adopted in 1902. It is similar to the state flag. It shows a mother pelican tearing some flesh from its own breast to feed its young. The state motto surrounds the pelican.

Almanac

General Facts

Nickname: Pelican State

Population: 4,468,976 (U.S. Census 2000)

Population rank: 22nd

Capital: Baton Rouge

Largest cities: New Orleans, Baton Rouge, Shreveport, LaFayette, and Lake Charles

Agriculture

Agricultural products: Rice, sugar, corn, cotton, potatoes, tobacco, crawfish

Climate

Average summer temperature: 81 degrees Fahrenheit (27 degrees Celsius)

Average winter temperature: 51 degrees Fahrenheit (11 degrees Celsius)

Average annual precipitation: 55 inches (140 centimeters)

General Facts

Area: 51,843 square miles (134,273 square kilometers)

Size rank: 31st

Highest point: Driskill Mountain, 535 feet (163 meters) above sea level

Lowest point: New Orleans, 5 feet (1.5 meters) below sea level

Crawfish

56

Magnolia

Symbols

Bird: Eastern brown pelican

Crustacean: Crawfish

Dog: Catahoula Leopard dog

Freshwater fish: White perch

Flower: Magnolia

Economy

Natural resources: Oil, natural gas, fishing, sulphur, lime, salt, lignite, seafood

Types of industry: Oil, natural gas, tourism, agriculture, papermaking, commercial fishing, seafood, shipbuilding

Symbols

Musical instrument: Diatonic accordion or "Cajun" accordion

Reptile: Alligator

Songs: "Give Me Louisiana" by Doralice Fontane

"You Are My Sunshine" by former governor Jimmie Davis, second state song

Tree: Bald cypress

Government

First governor: William Charles Cole Claiborne

Statehood: April 30, 1812 (18th state)

U.S. Representatives: 7

U.S. Senate: 2

U.S. electoral votes: 9

Parishes: 64

Timeline

State History

1715 Louis Juchereau de Saint-Denis establishes the first permanent settlement in Louisiana.

1718 New Orleans is founded.

1803 Thomas Jefferson purchases Louisiana Territory from France.

1812 Louisiana becomes a state.

1849 Capital city moves from New Orleans to Baton Rouge after a state-wide vote.

1862 Louisiana is occupied by Union troops.

1865 Convention of Colored Men is formed.

U.S. History

1620 Pilgrims establish Massachusetts Bay Colony.

1775–1783 American colonies fight for independence from Great Britain in the Revolutionary War.

1812–1814 The United States fights Great Britain in the War of 1812.

1861–1865 Union states fight Confederate states in the Civil War.

1866
Louisiana's Civil Rights Act passes.

1901
First oil field is discovered.

1935
Senator Huey P. Long is killed.

1950–1970
Desegregation process begins in Louisiana.

1984
World's Fair is held in New Orleans.

2002
Super Bowl XXXVI is played in New Orleans.

1914–1918
World War I is fought; the United States enters the war in 1917.

1929–1939
The United States experiences the Great Depression.

1939–1945
World War II is fought; the United States enters the war in 1941.

1964
U.S. Congress passes the Civil Rights Act, which makes discrimination illegal.

2001
Terrorists attack the Pentagon and the World Trade Center on September 11.

Words to Know

alluvial (ah-LOO-vee-ahl)—made from soil carried and left by a river

antebellum (an-tee-BELL-um)—refers to places, events, or things that took place before the Civil War

bayou (BYE-yoo)—a slow moving body of water

brackish (BRA-kish)—freshwater with saltwater added to it

Cajun (KAY-jun)—descendants of the Acadians from French Canada

gasohol (GASS-uh-hawl)—a fuel made from a blend of grain alcohol and gasoline; gasohol is safer for the environment than regular gasoline.

Napoleonic Code (nah-POLE–ee-ann-ick KOHD)—a means of settling legal issues developed in France; Louisiana courts follow the Napoleonic Code.

oxbow lake (OKS-boh LAKE)—a U-shaped lake formed when a river changes course

petroleum (peh-TROH-lee-um)—a thick, oily liquid found beneath the earth's surface

secede (si-SEED)—to split away from

sharecropper (SHAIR-krop-per)—a person who works a piece of land for food, shelter, and part of the crops grown

To Learn More

Bial, Raymond. *Cajun Home.* Boston: Houghton Mifflin, 1998.

Burgan, Michael. *The Louisiana Purchase.* We the People. Minneapolis: Compass Point Books, 2002.

Macaulay, Ellen. *Louisiana.* From Sea to Shining Sea. New York: Children's Press, 2003.

LaDoux, Rita. *Louisiana.* Hello U.S.A. Minneapolis: Lerner Publications, 2002.

Internet Sites

Track down many sites about Louisiana. Visit the FACT HOUND at *http://www.facthound.com*

IT IS EASY! IT IS FUN!
1) Go to *http://www.facthound.com*
2) Type in: 0736815864
3) Click on "FETCH IT" and FACT HOUND will find several links hand-picked by our editors.

Relax and let our pal FACT HOUND do the research for you!

Places to Write and Visit

Alligator Bayou Tours
35019 Alligator Bayou Road
Prairieville, LA 70769

Contemporary Arts Center
900 Camp Street
New Orleans, LA 70130

Louisiana Department of Culture, Recreation, and Tourism
P.O. Box 94361
Baton Rouge, LA 70804-9361

New Orleans Historic Voodoo Museum
724 Dumaine Street
New Orleans, LA 70116

Sam Houston Jones State Park
107 Sutherland Road
Lake Charles, LA 70611

Many Mardi Gras costumes include large hats decorated with beads, sequins, and colorful fabric.

Index

Acadians. See Cajuns
agriculture, 28–29, 41–42, 52
animals. See wildlife
antebellum mansions, 52
Armstrong, Louis, 50
Atchafalaya Swamp, 17

barrier islands, 15
Baton Rouge, 20, 21, 23, 24, 37
Battle of New Orleans, 24
Black Code, 27–28

Cajuns, 21, 22, 27, 47, 50
Charles III, King, 21
Civil War, 24–26, 52
Claiborne, William Charles Cole, 6, 24
Creole, 27, 47

desegregation, 30
Driskill Mountain, 13

economy, 13, 28, 29, 39–45
education, 30, 50–51
explorers, 18, 19–20
    La Salle, René-Robert Cavelier Sieur de, 18, 19–20
    Pineda, Alonso Alvarez de, 19
    Saint-Denis, Louis Juchereau de, 20

fishing, 39, 43–44, 45, 53
food, 44–45, 47–49
forestry, 29, 42–43
Free People of Color, 23, 26, 27, 48

government, 33–36, 37
Gulf of Mexico, 6, 9, 10, 13, 15

hurricanes, 15, 16

Jackson, Andrew, 24
Jefferson, Thomas, 23

Kemp's Ridley Sea Turtle, 14
Kisatchie National Forest, 12, 13

LaFitte, Jean, 24
Legasse, Emeril, 49
Long, Huey P., 37
Louis XIV, King, 19
Louis XV, King, 21
Louisiana Purchase, 23

Mardi Gras, 4, 5–6, 31, 45, 53, 62
Mississippi River, 6, 9, 10, 12, 19, 21, 38, 40, 41, 52, 53
music, 31, 45, 47, 50

Napoleon I, 22, 23, 34
Napoleonic Code, 34
Natchitoches, 20

New Orleans, 4, 5–6, 12, 21, 24, 25, 29, 30–31, 39, 44, 45, 46, 49, 50

parish, 33, 34
pelican, 6, 15
petroleum, 14, 15, 39–41
    gasohol, 40
    natural gas, 14, 40
    oil, 17, 29, 39–41, 51

Reconstruction, 26–28
Revolutionary War, 22–23

salt domes, 14–15, 39
Schwegmann, Melinda, 36
sharecropper, 28–29
steamboats, 52–53
sugarcane, 28, 41
Superdome, 31

Tabasco, 15, 42
tourism, 42, 44–45, 52
Treaty of Paris, 22

voodoo, 48

War of 1812, 24
wetlands, 9–17, 53
    bayous, 8, 10, 12, 15, 17, 44, 53
    marshes, 10, 13, 17
    oxbow lakes, 12
wildlife, 13, 15–17